EREN YAFF

CRYSTALS FOR BEGINNERS

The Ultimate Guide to Crystal Healing for Beginners, Discover All Information about Crystal Healing and How It Can Help You

Descrierea CIP a Bibliotecii Naţionale a României
EREN YAFF
    CRYSTALS FOR BEGINNERS. The Ultimate Guide to Crystal Healing for Beginners, Discover All Information about Crystal Healing and How It Can Help You / Eren Yaff. – Bucharest: Editura My Ebook, 2020
    ISBN

EREN YAFF

CRYSTALS FOR BEGINNERS

The Ultimate Guide to Crystal Healing for Beginners, Discover All Information about Crystal Healing and How It Can Help You

My Ebook Publishing House
Bucharest, 2020

TABLE OF CONTENTS

FOREWORD

Crystal therapy or crystal healing is a sort of vibrational medicine. Crystal therapy necessitates the application of crystals or gemstones to help healing.

Gemstones hold spiritual and healing attributes that may be tapped into an assortment of ways. Crystals may be carried or worn on the individual, or placed in a location where their therapeutic vibrations may be felt by whosoever is nearby. Healers likewise place stones on their clients' reclined bodies to equilibrate the chakras and aura.

Crystal Healing And The Power It Gives You

Learn How Crystal Healing Can Help You!

CHAPTER 1

WHAT'S BEHIND CRYSTAL HEALING

Synopsis

Crystal healing is a sort of healing that utilizes crystals or gemstones. The crystals are primarily placed on particular areas of the body named "chakras."

Chakra is a Hindu term implying spiritual energy. According to that teaching there are 7 general energy centers in the body, every one featuring a color affiliated with it.

A Little Beginning Info

A few crystal healers lay the same color crystals as the color of the chakras on the individual to heighten the flow of energy. Crystals are stated to guide the flow of energy to the individual in a certain part of the body and bring in balance to an individuals energy.

Ultimately, they're utilized to clean the individual from foul or damaging energy believed to induce a sickness. Driving out the defective spiritual energy eases the physical ailment. Crystals are utilized for physical, mental, emotional and spiritual healing.

Not only do individuals visit "crystal healers", in a few places, professional nurses are getting trained to utilize crystals for their patients. In addition, crystals may be worn, placed next to an individuals bed as they sleep, and in a few cases placed around an individuals bath.

The conceiver of crystal healing is nameless. All the same, this practice has been around for hundreds of years. Individuals have utilized amulets, magical stones, and gems all through history (although primarily in the eastern cultures). It's now making its way into the western culture, principally in the New Age and Occult causes.

Crystal healers contend that it really works; all the same, there's no concrete scientific evidence to establish that it really heals. Individuals state they've been healed and feel better, however these cases are broadly limited to personal testimonies.

A lot of the scientific world has brushed these testimonials off as a placebo effect, selective thinking, aspirant thinking, sympathetic magic, or communal reinforcement.

Crystal healers generally prefer clear quartz, because of its shape and color. All the same, as chakras have colors associated with every area, they might place the particular color crystal/gemstone on the same color chakras.

The crystals/gemstones are stated to have vibration frequencies that are shape stimulated, interconnecting the earth's and the persons energy field. The crystal is utilized to expand, or realign, human 'psychic' or cosmic energy by guiding vibration energy.

To maintain the crystal, it's laid in salt water or covered with table salt. Sustaining the crystal helps keeps it clean from "environmental unbalance." It's stated that it likewise needs to be recharged and actuated through assorted methods.

CHAPTER 2

RAMPING UP YOUR ENERGY

Synopsis

In the wake of extreme physical or emotional effort, the effects of weariness are certain to follow. Points of tiredness may last a couple of hours or, in extreme cases, a great deal longer.

And, in today's stressful times with tension pelting us from all sides – work (or deficiency thereof), loved ones, youngsters, physical sickness, finances – it might all feel overwhelming, and our bodies and minds will, sooner or later, come to the conclusion that they'll shut down!

Luckily, the battle over fatigue may be overcome.

More Power

There are a list of crystals that may help you and provide you that much-needed supercharge of energy. Broadly speaking, if faced with tiredness, pick out stones that are connected with the component of Fire. This component is energy personified. You'll discover, likewise, that stones ruled by fire are frequently ruled by the Sun or the planet Mars and are nearly always red in color.

Mars is frequently called the planet of warriors. If you wish to fight fatigue, you'll have to think like a warrior. That being stated, the crystals in that category are Ruby, Garnet, Red Jasper, and Amber. And as fatigue might likewise bring with it rounds of depression and/or insomnia, Amethyst and Green Aventurine are likewise on the list.

Ruby is a crimson crystal that's ruled by the component of Fire and the planet Mars. This potent energizer step-ups blood flow, heightens stamina, and presents you renewed energy. Utilize it on the sacral or root chakra. Raw, rough rubies are much less expensive and are perfect for this sort of healing. Reload rubies utilizing a soft cloth to wipe them down with and putting them on a windowsill at nighttime to be charged up by the stars.

Garnet is a burgundy-red stone that's likewise ruled by Fire and the planet Mars. Put on the root chakra, it may improve circulation as well and expand that sense of vitality you might be missing. This warming crystal may be worn or carried in a pocket (as with all of these crystals) and it may be recharged even on a mirky night.

Red Jasper is "the warrior rock". This red rock is, like Ruby and Garnet, likewise ruled by Fire and Mars. It's indispensable if you have to step-up stamina, heighten circulation and give an awesome boost of energy to the system.

It's affiliated with the root chakra and may be recharged by passing it through a red standard candle flame.

Amber, the fossilized leftovers of ancient tree resin, is affiliated with Fire and the Sun. This fiery, golden-orange "stone" reloads your energy levels by arousing a more favorable attitude. If your emotions are running rampant due to emotional overcharge, lay amber on the solar plexus or sacral chakra to counterbalance those emotional tensions. It may be reloaded by placing it on a sunshiny windowsill.

Amethyst is a quieting stone for those enduring fatigue ascribable to emotional overload. This purplish crystal is ruled by the component of Air and the planet Jupiter. It's thought of as an awesome healing stone for emotional weariness, insomnia and headaches. It likewise balances blood glucose levels and has been recognized to recharge other stones. Put it on your brow chakra or beneath your pillow at night. Naturally, it may be worn or carried. Reload amethyst by putting in moonlight, as this stone shouldn't be placed in direct sunlight.

Aventurine, while green, is a marvelous crystal for clearing off negativity, increasing optimism and affecting a more favorable outlook. It's a more gentle stimulating stone, but may still encourage a regenerated zest for life. It's an Earth stone and is ruled by Mercury. Aventurine is utilized on the heart chakra to quiet panic-attacks and nervousness affiliated with emotional fatigue. It may be recharged by placing it in amongst the leaves of a plant during the day.

A few of you might be wondering why the elements and planets are named with the crystal descriptions. Every element – Earth, Air, Fire and Water – and every planet – from the Sun to Pluto – correspond to assorted energies, emotions, attributes, colors, and so forth.

Fire, for instance, is affiliated with the color red and is utilized for physical strength, staying power, protection, energy and bravery. Water is blue and is utilized for healing, relaxation, rest, and psychic powers.

Earth is regulated by green and is utilized for grounding, peace, constancy, fertility, cash and gardening/agriculture. Air is yellow and is the component of communication, travel and all matters regarding the intellect.

Mentioned here were Mars, the Sun, Jupiter and Mercury. Mars is for bravery, passion, protection and strength and is governed likewise by red. The Sun deals with physical power, protection, healing and success and its color is golden or yellow. Jupiter is for meditation, spirituality, success and psychic cognizance and its color is purple. Mercury regulates communication, wiseness, self-reformation, study and travel, and its color is yellow.

A different area you might need a bit of a bracer is that afternoon burn out. You've ate lunch, its early afternoon and you're about prepared for a nap. This sort of afternoon slump may be alleviated with your crystals, instead of caffeinated drinks or sugary snacks.

Crystals that are going to hike up that afternoon slouch are Ruby, Amber and yes, Red Jasper. Ruby and Amber are reloading stones, and will jumpstart your system. A different one to try is Aventurine, which will add a little of optimism to the mix.

What if you're having difficulty catching some Z's? You're so wore down, you think you may sleep for a week, but your mind won't switch off. Cup of Chamomile Tea? Maybe some calming music and a little meditation? Go for it.

Rose Quartz and Amethyst will likewise bring a more relaxing sleep if placed beneath your pillow. These are quieting stones that will greatly help those with overtaxed brains and bouts of insomnia. A different stone to help you relax is Blue Lace Agate that, if held in your hand, will help your entire body relax.

It will likewise better the quality of your sleep, as will the crystal Iolite, which likewise helps with headaches, eyestrain and mental tension, by calming those overtaxed nerves.

So, whether you're a long-distance runner or simply running through the stress of day-after-day, I hope one or more of these crystals will help you to battle your fatigue and bring you serenity and energy.

CHAPTER 3

ABOUT AMETHYST

Synopsis

Amethyst is a gemstone frequently worn by healers, as it has the might to center energy. A healer will commonly wear various pieces of jewelry with amethysts set in silver, particularly an amethyst necklace.

The individual to be healed will have an Amethyst to hold while the healing is being executed. The healer will place a different piece of Amethyst on the area of the body in demand of healing, the heart or lungs commonly.

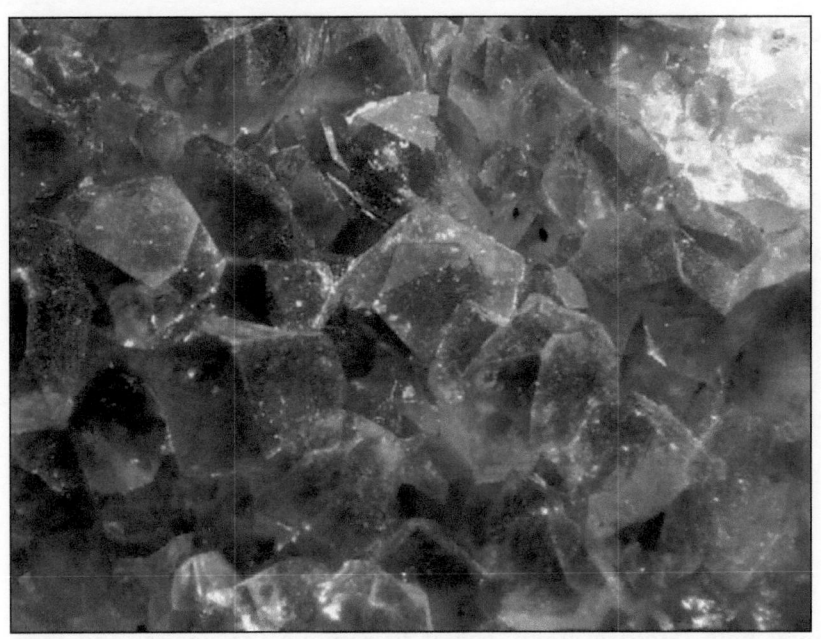

What This Stone Is Used For

Amethyst is utilized for issues in the blood and in breathing issues. Amethyst crystal clusters are utilized to keep the air and vitality in the home clean and favorable.

Amethyst clusters, points or various tumbled Amethysts laid in a window that gets sun most of the day are really beneficial to utilize in healing and to heal negativism in the home. Place Amethyst clusters, points or numerous tumbled Amethysts in moonlight and everybody in the home will be feeling less agitated. Utilizing an Amethyst as a meditation center will expand the positive spiritual feelings. Amethyst helps defeat fears and cravings. It likewise helps alleviate headaches.

Hold an amethyst stone in each hand when meditating. It's an excellent stone to better meditations as it helps better visualizations.

Place a couple of amethyst stones around the room where tempers might frequently be riled, like high stress occupations and business. It's a stone of peace and helps bestow love and happiness to all who utilize it.

If you discover yourself addicted to anything and you're working hard to check the addiction, an amethyst stone crystal may help. Hold a stone, ask it to remove the desire, and then draw strength out of the stone. It helps you do away with all sorts of addictions.

An Amethyst stone makes an awesome gift for anybody that works as a psychic or those that show psychic powers as it helps increase all forms of psychic abilities.

If you endure migraines, here's a simple crystal healing curative that has been known to help. Lie down and shut your eyes. Put an amethyst stone on your brow and attempt to relax and let the gemstone do its work.

Historically, muscle and joint traumas like sprains have been helped to heal quicker by putting an amethyst stone inside an elastic bandage that has been wound around the wounded area.

To assist breathing issues heal faster, along with any medications from the doctor, put an amethyst on the chest, between the lungs. Dependent on the harshness of the illness, you are able to actually tape a stone in place with a band aid and slumber with it in place.

To make an amethyst stone elixir, put one or more amethysts into a clear glass jar full of water. Let the water sit outside in the moon light for the whole night. The closer to the full moon the better on this one.

You are able to utilize amethyst water to help clear up blemishes and soften the skin. You may wash with it or utilize it as an ingredient in any clays or masks you might apply.

Wear an amethyst stone round your neck of carry one in your pocket to help fortify your bones.

If you discover yourself having issues sleeping at night and spend more time tossing and turning than really sleeping, place an amethyst stone beneath your pillow to help with insomnia.

To expand the number of dreams that you have and to help you recall your dreams when you awaken, utilize an elastic hair band as a head band around your fore head. Slip an amethyst stone beneath the band as it is known to help cause dreams.

Bury a little amethyst stone at every entrance to your house to guard against thieves. A cheap strand of amethyst chips works perfectly for this. Don't forget to bury a little beneath every window, as well as the doors. If you've a window that's far away from a place where you may bury the stones, like a window above a cement patio or porch, put a tumbled stone or little amethyst stone crystal formation on the windowpane.

Utilize the same technique above to protect against thieves to likewise keep evil from your household and will help keep all who wish you or your loved ones harm from attempting to come into your home.

If a man is seeking the perfect mate, somebody that will work with him on a journey to establish a life together, carry an amethyst stone in your pocket to draw in good women.

For the women, if you believe your man might be losing his interest in you, give him a gift of an amethyst stone to expand his attraction to you. This may be in the form of a ring or pendant, or even a worry stone to hold in his pocket will do fine.

To commune with your Spirit Guide or Higher Self, discover a peaceful time and place where you won't be interrupted. Carry an amethyst stone in each hand. Take a couple of deep breaths, shut your eyes feel the powers come from the amethyst. Let them come up your arm and into your head where you see them from inside your minds eye begin to glow. Invite your guide to come forward and talk with you. This helps you attune with your higher self.

Make an Amethyst Stone elixir and utilize it to bathe the parts of the body that are undergoing circulatory issues. It step-ups circulations in both the physical body and the etheric.

With the mad hectic world moving so quick around us, we frequently find ourselves strained beyond the capacity the human body was specified to take. Spend a couple of minutes absorbing the power of amethyst crystals to help mend the nervous system.

You've likely heard it stated, "You're your own worst enemy". Self- deceit, particularly when concerning matters of the heart induce more heart aches and chest pains than anything else mankind has ever mustered up. Amethyst stone crystals protect against self-deceit and let you view things the way they truly are.

CHAPTER 4

APATITE

Synopsis

It's frequently been stated, before you are able to change something, you have to accept it as it is. This is really true for most individuals where excess weight is a problem. An Apatite gemstone crystal is a multi-talented gemstone assisting us attune to our inner selves and take on the healing, communication, balancing and teaching it has to provide.

Slimming Down And More

Apatite gemstone is perfect for those with weight issues for it not solely aids in appetite suppression, but lets you look inside and see the truths inside ourselves. This is frequently required in a quest for weight loss so you are able to get to the root cause of overindulging.

The perfect gemstone for utilization on any of the chakras as it can both perk up under activity and calm down over activity and clear congestions in any of the chakras.

Apatite gemstone crystal aids in the development of psychic powers and helps you attune your mind, heart and soul to the spiritual forces that run throughout the universe.

Apatite gemstone helps bones to mend faster and stronger. It aids your body absorb calcium from the foods you consume, which helps to keep bones and teeth firm.

To help ease the hurting of arthritis, wrap the involved joint in an elastic bandage allowing it to hold one or more stones against the impacted joint. The apatite gemstone may help heal the painful sensation and heal the joint quicker.

To help lower hypertension, wear an apatite gemstone so it hangs just about on the heart. Wearing one on a chain is all right or if all else fails, pin a stone to the interior of your shirt.

If you realize inside you the tendency to let your emotions rule instead of logic, particularly in emergency type situations, apatite gemstone crystals may be your resolution. This gemstone will let calm prevail presenting you the time and power to let logic rule in the situation.

Wear one or more apatite crystals while executing any kind of creative work. It helps you to link up with your originative center and produce spectacular works.

Does shyness or doubt forbid you from enjoying yourself at parties or in additional social situations? An apatite gemstone may provide you the confidence to attempt contact with other people and provide you the feeling of security you require to shine at your best.

To expand your power to receive visions of the future, meditate with an apatite gemstone leaning against your 3rd eye chakras (somewhat above and between the eyebrows). Blue or purple colored apatite gems work best for this.

Require a little extra motivation to get the job finished? A gold or red apatite gemstone held during meditation may help you keep your mind centered on the subject at hand presenting you the desire to continue working till completion.

Produce an elixir by placing one or more apatite gemstones in a glass container of water and let it sit outside overnight, preferable under a full moon. This elixir may be drank to help beef up bones and heal and prevent joint pain.

CHAPTER 5

GREEN SERPENTINE

Synopsis

Serpentine is an earthling stone that helps meditation and spiritual exploration. It clears up the chakras and energizes the crown chakra, opens up psychic powers and helps us comprehend the spiritual basis of life.

Detox For The Body

This stone opens up fresh pathways for the Kundalini Energy to rise, aids in the retrieval of wiseness and regains memories of past lives. Serpentine assists you to be more in command of your life, corrects mental and emotional instabilities and assists the conscious direction of healing power towards trouble areas.

Physically, Serpentine mineral is exceedingly cleansing and detoxifying for the body and blood to assure longevity. It does away with parasites, aids calcium and magnesium absorption and treats hypoglycaemia and diabetes.

Light-Green Serpentine is a gentle, tender-natured stone that gets you into contact with angelic guidance. It gets at and integrates the past, present, future and is an awesome stone for past-life exploration.

This stone encourages compassion and forgiveness for yourself for what you experienced. Holding this stone leads you into the healing regions that exist in the between-lives state, so that healing that wasn't undertaken after a former life ended may be accomplished. I

This stone heals instabilities from past lives and clears up emotional baggage from old relationships. If placed on the Throat, it helps speaking of the past and resolves issues carried forward into the here and now. The stone is awesome to utilize when you want to confront anybody from your past, as it brings in a gentle touch to the meeting.

Physically, Light Green Serpentine is awesome for pain relief, particularly menstrual and muscular aches and annoyances.

CHAPTER 6

WHAT TURQUOISE CAN DO

Synopsis

Turquoise gemstone is the healing stone that attunes our physical selves to the greatest realms. It helps us to better comprehend ourselves and to bring our thoughts and emotions under command so we may see them get fruitful in our reality. You've but to stop and listen, be quiet and be prepared to hear the truth about whom and what you are. Simply then will you find your full power.

The Revered Blue/Green

Respected by the Native Americans as sacred, the turquoise gemstone soaks up negativity, transmuting it into valuable energy. It likewise helps you to become one with the cosmos. The real Turquoise meaning comes from the heart and the soul of the individual utilizing it.

The list of turquoise gem healing attributes is long and wide-ranging and the assortments of turquoise crystal shapes, sizes and colors that may be utilized are as wide-ranging as the individuals that utilize them.

Worn anyplace on the body, a turquoise gem healing stone will protect and bless the wearer. It's considered a hallowed stone in some cultures, personifying a gift from the gods.

A strand of turquoise gemstone crystal beads worn around the neck soaks up all negativity from the body and brain and helps you formulate your own innate powers. You are able to align your chakras by laying a turquoise stone on each of the chakra points for 3 to 5 minutes whilst the gem executes its work.

If you don't have seven turquoise stones, it might take a trifle longer, however laying a single stone on 1 chakra at one time for the same three to five minutes will still align your chakras for level best power.

A strand of turquoise beads utilized as a bracelet, necklace or even an anklet will help detoxify the body from alcoholic beverages, pollution, poison and radiation. The thought is to wear a circle of beads around one area of the body so as the blood flows backward and forward through the area, the turquoise may purify it.

Anybody that has issues with their lungs, throat or from asthma, may hang a turquoise gemstone from a cord or chain so it hangs immediately over the area causing the issue. This helps the gem energies get as close as possible to the trouble area and start the healing work even quicker.

Those suffering from depressive disorder may sleep with a turquoise gemstone to help lift the depression quicker.

Add a couple of turquoise crystals to a container of water and let it sit outside overnight where the moon may shine on it and then so the sun may shine on it during the day. That evening, pour the turquoise water into a bathtub of bath water, step in, sit down and let the healing energies work on your body.

This same healing elixir may be utilized to soak a sprained or pulled muscle, beef up the body so you may fight off viruses and infections, and assist damaged or cut tissues to mend.

35

For headaches, soak a cloth in the elixir and put on your brow till the pain disappears.

Have a speaking date coming up? Sleep with a turquoise crystal taped to your neck at night and wear one on a chain round your neck during the day to guarantee your ability to communicate with other people correctly.

CHAPTER 7

QUARTZ

Synopsis

In the pecking order of crystals utilized in spiritual healing nothing stands higher up than Quartz. The healing energies of quartz have long been recognized. Since the time of the fabled Atlantis no stone has been more revered for its crystal healing attributes than Quartz.

The Main One

To the shaman and metaphysical healer quartz is the quintessential curative stone. Quartz crystals posses all of the attributes the practitioner of Crystal Healing looks for.

Whether that's the Reiki Master, the Shaman or the acupuncturist who utilizes needles that have been coated with quartz. Even science realizes the unparalleled and astonishing abilities of Quartz Crystals.

The crystalline structure of quartz carries electricity and radio frequencies. It's why Quartz is utilized in radios and additional electronic devices. And why men of science are experimenting with Quartz and additional crystals as sources of possibly unlimited alternative energy.

The "Dilithum" Crystals that powered the Starship Enterprise, and the nearly magical crystals that were the basis of Kryptonian science in the Superman flicks, are likely not as implausible as it might seem, and were more than probably inspired by the really true energy transmutation powers of quartz crystals.

There are a lot of different sorts of Quartz Crystals, and every one has their own unequalled healing powers and impact different parts of the body and help with different ailments.

For instance Rose Quartz is utilized by crystal healers for headaches, the handling of heart issues and kidney disease. Although Clear Quartz is utilized to draw out pain, bring back clarity of consciousness, and to broadly amplify all curative energies.

However all Quartz Crystals have the power to accord with and realign the vibrations of the body, bringing back balance. That's what makes quartz crystals so efficient in healing. Most disease states, but particularly mental disorders, and neurological issues may be linked to some sort of "chemical" or "Neurotransmitter" instability. The influence of quartz crystals may mend these imbalances.

The electro-magnetic attributes of quartz are mostly due to the base of its crystalline anatomical structure being made up of Silica. Silica is a natural occurring glass. Silica is detected in some level in nearly every healing crystal, Chakra stone, or ritualistic gem. Silica likewise shares it chemical and molecular construction with Silicon, likewise known for its electro-magnetic attributes (does the name Silicon Valley mean anything?).

That's correct the same basic component that we rely on to communicate and transmit all of this data worldwide; that's allowing you to study this very page; might likewise help us communicate with and tap into the fabric of the cardinal energies of the universe.

Once more science and spirituality are not so aloof after all. It was Einstein himself who stated "The more I come to comprehend the universe, the more I'm convinced of the presence of a superior reasoning energy. There are 2 ways to live: you are able to live as if nothing is a miracle; or you are able to live as if everything is a miracle."

CHAPTER 8

BLOOD STONE

Synopsis

Formerly, bloodstone crystal was called Heliotrope. The word heliotrope is compiled of the Greek word for "the sun", helios and the Greek word for "to turn", trepein. The beginning historical uses of the stone were to induce changes in the weather. It was thought you place a bloodstone in water and let the water and the stone suck up the rays of the sun, it would induce a storm.

During the Middle Ages, the red spots on the stones were thought to be the blood of Jesus and the early Christians believed the stone held all the powers of Jesus, including the power to make the wearer un- seeable.

A few believe while Jesus was on the cross, his blood fell down on some jasper on the ground at the foot of the cross and this is how the bloodstone was produced. It was stated that the stones from that area held enormous power to cure almost anything and the gemstone was dedicated the nickname "The Martyr's Stone" because of this.

A hero's gemstone, frequently seen in armor breast plates and on swords for its power to arouse bravery in the most dangerous spots. Likewise considered to be a really strong healing stone allowing the wearer to remain impregnable in battle long after those around you have fallen down.

The Stone Of Blood

It advances creative thinking, self-expression, and artistry.

In the Middle Ages, bloodstone was ground into a powder, blended with honey and eggs and given to patients to heal tumors. A paste made of mashed bloodstone and honey was rubbed on cuts to stop surplus bleeding.

To help cure snakebite, affix a bloodstone to draw the poison out of the bite. Notice: This was an ancient utilization of the stone. I may do this while on my way to acquire medical help but to do this rather than getting medical help will be foolish.

The ancient Babylonians utilized engraved bloodstone in divinations. They utilized the way the assorted spots of red looked to tap into their psychic powers, producing an affect similar to a vision by following the array of the spots.

To purge your mind, body and soul, on the night of the full phase of the moon, find a place outdoor where you may lay under the moons light.

Put a stone on your forehead and as you lay there, visualize the moon's power entering your body, filling it with perfect white light, as your body fills, see all the negativism, illness and tension leaving from your body, leaving from the rear of your body and sinking into the ground under you.

Ancient Egyptians utilized bloodstone magic to assist them in battles. They utilized magical empowered stones as amulets for the warriors to expand their personal strength.

To turn "invisible" to your foes, wear or carry a bloodstone and visualize a cloak of power emanating from the stone and enfolding around you, making you un-seeable to those you don't want to see you.

Athletes may utilize a bloodstone amulet to help expand their strength and speed. Wear or carry a stone and visualize its power entering your body and inducing your muscles to become firmer (or faster).

This same magic may be utilized by anybody in need of bravery to get through a situation. Simply envision the powers entering the body and presenting you the aspects that you require.

If you know of somebody that tends to be a bit too "me" oriented, give them a gift of a heliotrope. It helps them to see how matters affect not just them but other people around them or even the whole world.

Hold a bloodstone in your hands with meditations designed to help you connect with your preceding lives. Once you've entered the meditative state, turn your thoughts backward to a time before your birth and let the images guide you to sights of your prior lives.

Keep one or more bloodstones on your desk or work table to help expand your business and riches. Even those that don't run their own business may benefit by letting the stone draw in additional sources of money into their lives.

As a healing stone, a bloodstone is utilized by healers to help with any sort of blood disorders. This includes but isn't limited to anemia, circulatory issues and Lupis.

Wearing of carrying a bloodstone helps to beef up the immune system, clean toxins from the liver and kidney and purify the bone marrow. Makes and awesome stone for women as it helps to alleviate both menstrual and menopausal symptoms.

CHAPTER 9

CHOOSING THE RIGHT CRYSTALS

Synopsis

Here is an easy procedure to identify which crystal will work best for your particular goal.

How To

- Distinctly identify your aim

- Seek a few crystal assortments that appear to support your goal (in a book, net, from a professional, and so forth.).

- Select a particular specimen that provides vibrational match to your frequency.

That final part is best achieved by holding the crystal in your hand or thinking about holding it (if you're purchasing online for instance) and say your purpose: "I wish to slim down." Always say the purpose in an affirmatory sentence (so do not say: "I wish to quit feeling angry").

Affirmative sentences allow the flow of energy (which is what you require), while damaging sentences trigger resistors. Shut your eyes while you say your purpose so you are able to center inward.

If you're more in-tuned with your emotions, seek a great feeling (light, tingly, happy, grinning, great memories spring to mind, laughing are all great).

If you're more in-tuned with your body, you are able to utilize muscle testing: balance yourself upright and let your body "hover" and let it fall in the way it wishes. If you fall frontwards, it means you have a great match. If you fall rearwards, you don't. There are a lot of different ways to utilize muscle testing for this intent, this is a simple one.

Once you've discovered the crystal, make a conscious conclusion to let yourself be open to its influence. In order to interact with the tangible world, we frequently have to shut down our receptivity to remote influences.

That may lead to a generalized shutdown where all influences are barricaded. You may discover yourself inadvertedly fighting the crystal's influence.

One last thing you are able to do to facilitate the influence procedure is to place your crystal close to a little water fountain. Don't place them in the water, as the mineral deposits may damage them.

But anyplace near the fountain will do. This lets the really powerful chi of the water propagate the vibrational frequency of the crystal throughout your home or office.

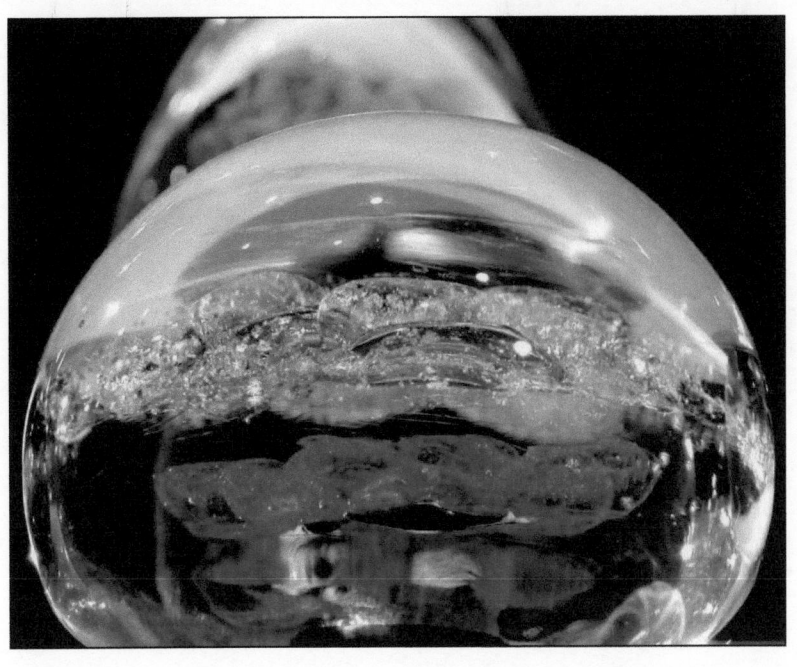

Wrapping Up

When you look for the help of a crystal, you're enlisting a potent ally to "raise" your vibrational frequency. Regardless what the crystal is utilized for, its desired effect is always a gain in your vibrational frequency. We frequently crave particular crystals because we have a great "vibrational match" with them. This vibrational match implies that proximity to this crystal elevates our vibrational frequency, therefore making us feel "great."

Choosing a crystal for a particular purpose is an awesome way to help yourself without having to commit much energy to it. The proximity of the crystal is perpetually affecting your own frequency, maneuvering you upward towards your goal. Likewise, a crystal that doesn't have a great match is perpetually draining you by lowering your vibrational frequency. Therefore, picking out the right crystal is of essential importance.

There are a lot of books that depict crystals and their usage, yet most of them disagree on precise properties. This makes perfect sense if you think about that different crystals of the same family have assorted properties, and likewise that individuals will respond to them differently. But with the knowledge you have gotten here you should have a starting point.

Printed by Libri Plureos GmbH in Hamburg,
Germany